C000103084

Vegetarian Recipes For One To Lower Blood Pressure

Polly Fielding

Copyright © 2018 Polly Fielding

All rights reserved.

ISBN: 9781791552787

Other books by Polly Fielding

Delicious Vegetarian Diabetic Meals For One

Single Serving Vegetarian Recipes To Soothe Arthritis

Single Serving Recipes To Soothe Arthritis

The 5:2 Diet Made eZy

The 5:2 Vegetarian Diet Made eZy

Mindfulness For The 5:2 Diet

Moments of Mindfulness

Time for Mindfulness

Nurturing Compassion

A Veritable Smorgasbord

Missing Factor

Going In Seine

Breaking The Silence

Letting Go (a trilogy comprising the three books below)

And This Is My Adopted Daughter

A Mind To Be Free

Crossing The Borderline

www.pollyfielding.com

To my good friends Shirley and Stewart

CONTENTS

ACKNOWLEDGMENT

My grateful thanks to Hemini Bharadia, Marketing
Manager at Blood Pressure UK. Her help and advice are
really appreciated

Introduction

High blood pressure can kill. And It affects around a quarter of adults worldwide.

Many people are completely oblivious to the fact that their blood pressure is too high because mostly they don't have any symptoms.

Worryingly, the number of sufferers is continuing to rise, often with devastating consequences. Uncontrolled high blood pressure (also called hypertension) has the potential, over time, to cause a fatal heart attack or stroke without a person having known that they were living with a ticking time bomb. It's the greatest single known risk factor for cardiovascular disease. As well as increasing the risk for heart attacks and strokes it can also result in chronic kidney disease, vascular dementia and heart failure.

The good news is that this scary scenario is not inevitable. Your lifestyle choices make a huge difference to your state of health. The food you eat, what you drink, physical activity - all these can dramatically affect your health.

Your diet is really important; it can contribute to raising or lowering your blood pressure and it's something over which, with the appropriate measures, you can have control. Some foods, such as those containing an appreciable percentage of potassium, are particularly helpful to include in your meals, whilst others with sugar, lots of saturated fat or salt content are best avoided. Herbs and spices can make a dish extremely tasty without the need for salt. The recipes in this book incorporate all the kinds of ingredients that enable you to prevent suffering from high blood pressure, or to lower it if it's already raised.

My aim is to encourage you to make small but significant changes to the way you live, especially to eat healthy meals so that you can keep your blood pressure down and make the very most of your life.

Understanding Blood Pressure

What is blood pressure?

Your heart keeps you alive by pumping blood through arteries around your body. The force of circulating blood against the walls of your arteries is called blood pressure. Unless this pressure is measured you are not usually aware of its strength, either normal or abnormal.

Why do you need to be aware of your blood pressure?

Because regular checks - at least once a year over the age of 40 - can alert you and your doctor to any problems with blood pressure. Left untreated, high blood pressure can remain symptomless until it results in a medical emergency such as a stroke or heart attack before you realise that something is seriously wrong.

How is blood pressure checked?

The doctor or nurse at your GP's surgery will use a device whose correct medical name is a complicated-sounding and practically unpronounceable word: sphygmomanometer. In the time it takes to articulate this word correctly, you will have had a cuff wrapped around your upper arm, painlessly inflated and blood pressure and pulse readings recorded. These measurements, obtained from what is more commonly known as a blood pressure monitor or gauge, indicate whether or not any further action is necessary.

So what do these measurements mean?

The higher number on the monitor shows your systolic pressure - the maximum force on your artery walls when your heart is pumping blood; whilst the lower number - which is the diastolic - indicates the minimum pressure on artery walls when your heart is resting between beats.

The numbers are followed by the letters mmHg, which refer to millimetres of mercury rising up a glass tube to measure pressure. Some doctors still prefer to use this traditional, very accurate device. However, nowadays an electronic monitor is more commonly used, though the measurement scale remains the same despite the absence of mercury.

What is the ideal range for blood pressure?

Although for the systolic 120-140 mmHg and for diastolic 70-90 mmHg are broadly viewed as acceptable, the optimum numbers are 90 - 120 for the systolic and 60-80 for the diastolic. Generally speaking, the lower the numbers, the better the outlook for your health.

Some people, however, have hypotension (low blood pressure), where their BP readings are frequently lower than the ideal range. This is rarely a problem, particularly if there are no accompanying symptoms. Their doctor might investigate to determine any possible reasons for this but it could quite simply be their normal, healthy state - we are all different in so many ways!

Far more common and worrying is hypertension (high blood pressure) where readings consistently register above 140 over 90 and the earlier this is picked up the better the outcome for your long- term health and longevity.

Does my blood pressure stay the same?

No, everyone's blood pressure fluctuates naturally to some extent. And there are several things that can affect it such as very hot or cold weather, your state of health and your level of physical activity; also short-term stressful situations can cause your blood pressure to spike - doctors are well aware that some patients get rather nervous during an initial visit to them, which can lead to a higher than usual reading. This even has its own term - 'white coat syndrome' - though your GP is unlikely to be wearing one of these.

What causes hypertension?

We do not know exactly what causes high blood pressure; for most people, there may be no single cause. We do know, however, that your lifestyle can affect your risk of developing it. You are at a higher risk if you:-

- eat too much salt

- don't eat enough fruit and vegetables

- are not active enough

- are overweight

- drink too much alcohol

- smoke

Additional factors that can raise your chances of developing it are: -

- chronic insomnia

- cholesterol

- some medications, whether prescribed or over the counter,

- high levels of stress - although there is no definitive proven link between stress and long-term hypertension, your body produces a surge of hormones when you're in a stressful situation. These hormones temporarily increase your blood pressure by causing your heart to beat faster and your blood vessels to narrow. Short-term stress-related spikes in your blood pressure, added up over time, may put you at risk of developing high blood pressure. Moreover, other behaviours linked to stress - such as overeating, drinking alcohol and poor sleeping habits - may cause high blood pressure.

There are, though, some factors that increase your risk of developing high blood pressure that you cannot control. These include:-

- age: as you get older, the cumulative effects of an unhealthy lifestyle can build up and your blood pressure can increase.

- ethnic origin: people from African-Caribbean and South Asian communities are at greater risk than other people of high blood pressure.

- family history: you are at greater risk if other members of your family have, or have had, high blood pressure.

Some people may have high blood pressure that is linked to another medical condition, such as kidney problems or diabetes. For these people, treating the related medical problem adequately may also bring their blood pressure back down to a normal level.

How is it treated?

It might possible to isolate a specific reason for your elevated blood pressure and find an obvious remedy; for example: giving up smoking or cutting back on alcohol. If you suspect it could be due to medication your doctor may be able to adjust the dosage or recommend an alternative drug.

Other risks, such as genetics, cannot in themselves be altered. However, that does not mean that hypertension, with its potentially devastating consequences, is inevitable.

Your doctor can arrange for a series of tests and might also lend you a twenty-four hour blood pressure monitor to wear to get an overall picture. You could also be referred to a specialist for further investigations. Certain lifestyle changes will undoubtedly be advised and medication prescribed if necessary.

How can you prevent/control hypertension?

You can definitely help to lower your blood pressure - and your risk of stroke and heart attack - by making some lifestyle changes. Indeed there's a lot that you can do, not only in terms of controlling this serious condition if you have it already, but also in many cases to avoid developing it in the first place.

Thanks to extensive scientific research, much is now known about how the way we live can impact on our state of health and the likelihood, or not, of becoming prone to suffering from a number of ailments in the long run.

Basically, by making positive changes to nutrition, exercise, weight and alcohol consumption, you can ensure that you have the best possible chance of living a longer, healthier, happier life.

It's not rocket science to conclude that the manner in which you treat your body is going to affect its continued healthy functioning. If you want to keep your car running efficiently you look after it, you get it regularly serviced and checked over. Similarly, your body will respond to being well cared for on a regular basis.

A moderate degree of daily physical exercise is excellent

for strengthening the heart. And if your heart is stronger it can pump blood with less effort, which decreases pressure on your artery walls and consequently lowers your blood pressure. There are several types of small pedometer you can buy to attach to clothing or wear on your wrist; these record the number of steps you take each day – 10,000 is the suggested number (four to five miles depending on the length of your stride). Although this may sound a lot, it's surprising how much small changes can move you towards your goal. Going up the stairs instead of using an escalator, getting off the bus a couple of stops before your destination to walk the remaining distance and doing housework are all steps in the right direction.

Finding ways to reduce your stress levels can greatly improve your general health, including your blood pressure. You can definitely lighten your mood and modify your response to stressful situations by practising any of the widely-available, easily-accessible, calming techniques such as relaxation, mindfulness, meditation, yoga, qi gong ...

What you consume on a daily basis is one of the most important and effective ways of preventing or controlling hypertension.

Drinking enough water - around eight glasses each day - is an excellent way to help keep your blood pressure down naturally. Also, your heart will benefit from keeping to, or below, the recommended maximum units of alcohol, having a few alcohol-free days every week and not binge drinking.

Where diet is concerned, most people are aware that a high sodium intake raises blood pressure. It's not enough though to merely cut out table salt as there are many products, such as processed food, which contain an excess. So when shopping, it's worth checking labels for sodium content.

Eating meals rich in potassium is another surefire move to keep your blood pressure at a healthy level. Whole grains, nuts, yogurts, vegetables such as fresh leafy greens, potatoes and avocados and fruit such as bananas, apricots and kiwi are all rich in this essential mineral. By including some of these in your daily diet you can make a huge difference to keeping your weight as well as your blood pressure in balance.

All the recipes in this book are designed to help you improve your blood pressure and make your meals a pleasurable experience.

Enjoy!

Breakfasts

Sweet Potato Treat

Ingredients

1 medium sweet potato

4 tbsp fat free vanilla yogurt

2 apricots, halved & de-stoned

2 tbsp granola

¼ tsp cinnamon

Method

- Preheat grill to high
- Cut four slices of sweet potato, approx ¼ inch thick
- Put slices onto foil-lined grill pan & grill for approx 5 min each side, until softened & lightly browned
- Remove slices & place on serving plate
- Top each one with some yogurt
- Place an apricot half, cut side up, on each slice
- Sprinkle granola into apricots
- Complete with a touch of cinnamon

Fruity Couscous

Ingredients

120ml (4 fl.oz) semi-skimmed milk

56g (2 oz) couscous

56g (2 oz) blueberries

56g (2 oz) raisins

Stevia (optional)

Method

- Microwave milk until hot (approx 40 seconds depending on your microwave)
- Stir couscous into milk & allow to stand for 5 min
- Add blueberries & raisins
- Sprinkle on stevia to taste
- Enjoy your breakfast!

Pear & Ginger Smoothie

Ingredients

1 soft, juicy pear

1 tsp clear honey

2 oranges

1 small piece of ginger root, to taste, finely chopped

Method

- Preheat the grill to medium
- Cut the pear in half, removing core & stalk
- Place the halves flesh side up on a baking tray
- Brush with honey
- Grill for about 7 minutes until the flesh is softened & the honey caramelises
- Squeeze the oranges & put the juice in a blender
- Add the pears & ginger & blend thoroughly
- Pour into a glass to serve

Spiced Fruit Salad

Ingredients

56g (2 oz) melon

56g (2 oz) strawberries

56g (2 oz) grapes

56g (2 oz) apple

56g (2 oz) blackberries

56g (2oz) mango chunks, fresh or frozen

¼ tsp mixed spice

Method

- Cut melon into small chunks
- Slice strawberries
- Halve grapes
- Core & slice apple
- Put all fruit into a serving bowl
- Add mixed spice & stir well
- Serve at room temperature or chilled

Spicy Peach Oatmeal

Ingredients

100ml (3½ fl.oz) water

28g (1 oz) oats

1 tsp nutmeg

1 tsp cinnamon

1 small peach, de-stoned & sliced

1 tsp stevia

14g (½ oz) chopped pecan nuts

Method

- Boil the water in a saucepan over medium heat
- Stir in oats, nutmeg & cinnamon
- Cook until oats begin to thicken (approx 4 min)
- Add peach slices & stevia & cook for a further 30 seconds
- Transfer to a bowl & sprinkle pecans over

Tasty Chia & Raspberry

Ingredients

150ml (5 fl oz) coconut milk, unsweetened

112g (4 oz) raspberries

2 tbsp chia seeds

$^1/_3$ tsp stevia

4 strawberries, halved

Method

- Combine milk & raspberries in blender until smooth
- Pour into airtight container & stir in chia seeds & stevia
- Seal with lid & put into fridge overnight
- Your breakfast awaits you in the morning – just top with strawberry halves
- Bon appétit!

Banana Pancakes

Ingredients

1 ripe banana

1 large free range egg

¼ tsp cinnamon

¼ tsp vanilla extract

1 tbsp olive oil

1 tbsp fat free vanilla yogurt

1 large kiwi fruit, peeled & sliced

Method

- Mash banana with fork
- Add egg, cinnamon & vanilla extract & mix well
- Grease frying pan with oil & warm on low heat
- Pour in a little mixture at a time to make 3 small pancakes
- Brown pancakes on both sides
- Transfer to serving plate & top each one with yogurt & kiwi slices

Heart-Healthy Smooth Breakfast

Ingredients

70g (2½ oz) cucumber, peeled

120ml (4 fl.oz) unsweetened almond milk

Flesh of ½ medium avocado

1 large lime, peeled & sliced

112g (4 oz) of organic silken tofu

100g (3 ½ oz) frozen broccoli

84g (3 oz) baby spinach

½ cup ice

¼ tsp stevia

Method

- Put all above ingredients into a blender & blitz on high speed until smooth
- Transfer to a bowl & it's ready to eat

Hearty Overnight Almond, Seed & Berry Brekky

Ingredients

42g (1½ oz) chia seeds

10g ($^1/_3$ oz) hemp seeds

10g ($^1/_3$ oz) almond flakes

1 tbsp agave syrup

4 cardamom pods

200ml (6 ½ fl.oz) almond milk

1 tsp goji berries

Method

- Put seeds, flakes, syrup, pods into a bowl
- Pour on milk & mix thoroughly, cover & place in fridge
- The next morning take out cardamom pods
- Top with the goji berries before serving

Oats with Fruit & Nuts

Ingredients

28g (1 oz) oats

100ml (3½ fl.oz) semi-skimmed milk

1 small banana

112g (4 oz) apricots

1 tbsp low fat natural yogurt

Pinch of cinnamon

1 tbsp chopped walnuts

Method

- Mash banana in a bowl
- Chop apricots
- Put oats & milk into a saucepan, heat gently & cook until thickened
- Stir cooked oats into banana
- Top with yogurt
- Sprinkle on chopped apricots, cinnamon & nuts

Strawberry French Toast

Ingredients

2 eggs

60ml (2 fl.oz) unsweetened almond milk

½ tsp vanilla essence

Pinch of cinnamon, to taste

2 slices wholegrain bread

1 tbsp olive oil

6 strawberries, sliced

Method

- Crack eggs into a bowl & whisk

- Pour in milk & essence

- Add cinnamon & stir well

- Dip each bread slice in the mixture to cover both sides thoroughly

- Heat oil gently in large non-stick frying pan

- Add bread slices & cook, turning each one over so that they are golden brown on both sides

- Transfer to serving plate

- Garnish each piece with strawberry slices

Fruit & Nut Muesli

Ingredients

84g (3 oz) oats

45ml (1½ fl.oz) pure apple juice

¼ tsp ground cinnamon

28g (1 oz) wheat germ

120ml (4 fl.oz) semi-skimmed milk

1 small green apple

1 tbsp natural low fat yogurt

½ small kiwi fruit

1 tsp honey

28g (1 oz) blueberries

28g (1 oz) toasted almond flakes

Method

- Put oats, apple juice, cinnamon, wheat germ & milk into an airtight container & mix thoroughly.

- Seal & place overnight in fridge

- In the morning, spoon mixture into a bowl

- Core, grate & stir in apple

- Peel & chop kiwi

- Spoon yoghurt over & top with kiwi, honey, blueberries & almond flakes

Fibre-Filled Breakfast

Ingredients

1 tbsp almond butter

2 tbsp almond flour

180ml (6 fl.oz) unsweetened almond milk

56g (2 oz) shredded unsweetened coconut

1 tsp vanilla extract

Stevia or pure honey to taste

2 apricots, de-stoned & chopped

Chopped pecan nuts

Method

- Put almond butter into saucepan & melt over low heat

- Stir in flour

- Pour in the almond milk, add coconut & vanilla extract & stir continuously until your desired consistency is reached

- Spoon into bowl

- Sweeten with honey or stevia as required

- Top with apricots & pecan nuts

Carrot & Apple Pick-Me-Up

Ingredients

120ml (4 fl.oz) carrot juice

60ml (2 fl.oz) pure apple juice

2 tbsp natural yogurt

1 small apple, cored & chopped

¼ tsp ground cinnamon

 2 Ice cubes

Method

- Put all ingredients into blender
- Whizz until mixed thoroughly
- Pour into glass to serve

Melony Start

Ingredients

¼ cantaloupe melon

112g (4 oz) fat-free, Greek-style natural yogurt

1 tbsp crushed mixed nuts

4 mint leaves, chopped

Method

- Scoop seeds out of melon
- Place melon on serving plate & cut flesh evenly, leaving attached to rind
- Scoop yogurt evenly over
- Sprinkle on nuts
- Decorate with mint before eating each piece mindfully

Scrambled Egg, Spring Onion & Avocado

Ingredients

1 slice wholegrain sourdough bread

½ avocado

1 large free range egg

1 tbsp unsweetened almond milk

Freshly ground black pepper, to taste

1 tsp olive oil spread

1 tbsp spring onions, chopped

Method

- Toast sourdough bread
- Mash avocado & spread it evenly over toast
- Whisk egg, milk & black pepper
- Heat olive oil spread in a small saucepan, on low heat
- Pour egg mixture into saucepan & cook until scrambled, stirring continuously

- Spoon scrambled egg over avocado

- Sprinkle spring onions over

Tortilla with Potassium-Rich Filling

Ingredients

112g (4 oz) natural, fat free yogurt

1 apple, cored & sliced

1 small banana, sliced

28g (1 oz) blueberries

1 tsp chopped mixed nuts

1 whole grain tortilla

Method

- Spoon yogurt into a bowl
- Add apple slices
- Stir in banana slices
- Add blueberries
- Mix in the nuts
- Cut the tortilla open to make a pocket
- Scoop yogurt mixture into tortilla & place on serving plate

Malted Banana Toast with Orange Juice

Ingredients

2 slices malt loaf

1 large banana

1 tsp pure honey

2 oranges

Method

- Toast bread slices
- Slice banana
- Cover each piece of toast with banana slices
- Drizzle honey over
- Squeeze oranges & pour juice into a glass
- Eat & drink slowly - delicious!

Speedy Breakfast

Ingredients

112g (4 oz) cottage cheese

56g (2 oz) blueberries

1 tsp chia seeds

Method

- Scoop cottage cheese into a bowl
- Stir in blueberries
- Add chia seeds & stir again
- It's ready already!

Sweet Potato Frittata

Ingredients

2 tbsp olive oil

Frozen mixed vegetables of choice (amount as desired)

3 eggs

1 tsp Italian seasoning

½ tsp dried oregano

Freshly ground pepper to taste

140g (5 oz) cooked & diced sweet potato

Method

- Heat oil in frying pan on medium high heat
- Fry mixed vegetables gently
- Meanwhile, whisk eggs together with all seasonings
- When vegetables are tender, add sweet potato
- Pour in egg mixture & spread evenly
- Reduce heat & cover until cooked

Mediterranean Omelette

Ingredients

Flesh of ½ avocado

1 tsp finely chopped onion

Dash of chilli sauce

1 tbsp olive oil

2 medium free range eggs

1 tbsp semi-skimmed milk

½ tsp fresh coriander, chopped

Sprig of parsley

1 large vine tomato, sliced

Method

- Scoop avocado flesh into bowl & mash
- Mix in onion & chilli sauce
- Heat oil gently in non-stick frying pan
- Whisk eggs milk & coriander thoroughly & pour into frying pan

- Cook on medium heat until egg just begins to set

- Spoon avocado mixture evenly onto half of omelette

- Ease around edge of omelette with a spatula before folding in half

- When base is golden brown, slide omelette onto serving plate

- Garnish with parsley

- Surround with tomato slices & savour each mouthful

Poached Egg with Tomato & Kale

Ingredients

Splash of vinegar

1 tsp olive oil

56g (2 oz) fresh kale

¼ tsp chilli flakes

1 small garlic clove

1 large free range egg

1 slice whole grain bread

10g ($^1/_3$ oz) feta cheese

28g (1 oz) cherry tomatoes

Method

- Fill saucepan with water, add vinegar & place on medium heat until water is simmering

- Chop kale & crush garlic

- Heat oil gently in a frying pan & add kale, garlic & chilli flakes

- Cook, stirring occasionally, until kale wilts &

shrinks (approx 3 min)

- Meanwhile, stir simmering water rapidly to swirl, crack egg & slip it gently into water until egg white is just set & yolk still runny, about 2 min

- Toast bread slice & transfer to serving plate

- Remove egg with slotted spoon & place on middle of toast

- Surround egg with kale mixture

- Crumble feta & sprinkle over

- Arrange cherry tomatoes around toast & tuck in

Peanut-Buttered Banana Toast

Ingredients

1 slice wholemeal bread

1 tbsp peanut butter

1 small banana, sliced

6 raspberries

Method

- Toast the bread & spread peanut butter onto one side

- Place banana slices over

- Add raspberries & munch mindfully!

Mushrooms with Spinach & Goat Cheese

Ingredients

2 tbsp olive oil

200g (7 oz) mushrooms, chopped

100g (3½ oz) baby spinach leaves, chopped

1 sprig rosemary

Freshly ground pepper

100g (3½ oz) goat cheese

1 slice sourdough bread

Method

- Heat oil gently in frying pan
- Add mushrooms, spinach, rosemary & pepper
- Sauté until the mushrooms & spinach are cooked, approx 4 min
- Transfer to serving plate
- Slice cheese & arrange over mushrooms & spinach
- Serve with sourdough bread

Fresh Fruit Filler

Ingredients

28g (1 oz) blueberries

2 medium plums, de-stoned & chopped

2 apricots, halved

1 satsuma, segmented

6 seedless grapes

1 small banana, sliced

Small wedge honeydew melon, diced

84g (3 oz) strawberries, sliced

Juice of a lemon, freshly squeezed

Stevia to taste

Method

- Put fruit into a serving bowl
- Pour lemon juice over & mix thoroughly
- Sprinkle with a little stevia
- Notice each different flavour as you eat it

Lunches

Veggie Filled Muffin

Ingredients

1 small onion

½ small green pepper

1 Portobello mushroom

2 tbsp olive oil

Flesh of ½ avocado

½ small garlic clove, crushed

Freshly ground black pepper, to taste

1 wholemeal muffin

Method

- Cut onion & green pepper into slices

- Roughly chop mushroom

- Heat oil in non-stick frying pan over medium heat

- Slice muffin into half on serving plate

- Add onion, pepper & mushroom to pan & cook

until tender, stirring frequently, 3-4 min

- Meanwhile, mash avocado in a bowl, add crushed garlic & ground pepper & mix thoroughly

- Spread one half of muffin with avocado mixture

- Spoon onion, peppers & mushroom onto avocado mash

- Cover with remaining muffin half & enjoy!

Minty Carrot & Beetroot with Seeds

Ingredients

1 carrot

1 cooked beetroot

1 tbsp fresh mint, chopped

1 tbsp fresh parsley, chopped

¼ lemon

2 tsp olive oil

14g (½ oz) pumpkin seeds

14 g (½ oz) sunflower seeds

Couple of unsalted wholegrain rice cakes

Method

- Peel & grate carrot & beetroot
- Put carrot, beetroot, mint & parsley into a bowl
- Add juice of lemon
- Stir in oil
- Dry-roast seeds in heated frying pan, over

medium heat, shaking continuously until golden brown, approx 3 min

- Tip seeds into bowl with carrot, beetroot & herbs & toss well to combine

- Serve with rice cakes

Asparagus Omelette

Ingredients

56g (2 oz) asparagus

2 spring onions

56g (2 oz) frozen peas

2 large eggs

2 tsp semi-skimmed milk

Freshly ground black pepper, to taste

2 tsp chopped chives

2 tsp chopped parsley

1 tbsp olive oil

Sprig of parsley

Method

- Put saucepan of water on to boil
- Meanwhile, chop asparagus & spring onions thinly
- Put asparagus & peas into boiling water & cook until asparagus is tender, approx 5 min

- Whisk eggs with milk & ground pepper

- Drain asparagus & peas & add to egg mixture

- Add in chives, spring onion & parsley & stir well

- Heat oil in non-stick frying pan on medium heat & pour egg mixture into it

- Cook until eggs are nearly set, then lower heat & continue to cook until surface of omelette is firm

- Use spatula to fold one half over & slide omelette onto a serving plate

- Garnish with parsley

Tasty Tortilla

Ingredients

1 large red pepper

1 medium onion

2 tbsp olive oil

84g (3 oz) frozen sweetcorn, defrosted

112g (4 oz) cooked kidney beans

2 tbsp no added salt salsa

1 wholewheat tortilla wrap

Method

- Chop onion & pepper into small chunks

- Heat oil in non-stick frying pan over medium heat

- Sauté onion & pepper until soft, 4-5 min, adding sweetcorn, kidney beans & salsa for approx 1 min until warmed through, stirring continuously

- Warm tortilla in microwave for a few secs

- Place on serving plate & spoon on cooked mixture

- Fold carefully & it's a wrap!

Onion, Garlic, Tofu & Parsley Bruschetta

Ingredients

1 slice wholemeal bread

2 slices onion, chopped

1 clove garlic, crushed

Pinch of paprika

56g (2 oz) soft silken tofu, drained

1 tsp freshly chopped parsley

Few drops of olive oil

Method

- Toast bread
- Meanwhile, put onion, garlic, paprika, tofu, parsley & oil into a bowl & mix well
- Place toast on a plate & spoon mixture over it to cover
- Savour each tasty bite

Vegetable Soup

Ingredients

1 onion

1 stick celery

1 carrot

300ml (10 fl.oz) very low salt vegetable stock

2 cooked beetroots

1 tsp olive oil

Pinch freshly ground black pepper

Couple of matzos

Method

- Chop onion, celery & carrot

- Bring vegetable stock to boil in a saucepan

- Add vegetables & simmer until soft, stirring occasionally

- Meanwhile, grate beetroot

- Add beetroot & oil to saucepan & simmer for about 2 more min, until heated through

- Season with pepper

- Cool slightly before pouring soup into blender

- Blend on high setting until smooth, adding a little water, if required

- Reheat if necessary

- Transfer to a bowl & serve with matzos

Quick Apricot Lunch

Ingredients

4 apricots

1 tbsp olive oil

28g (1 oz) rocket

2 tsp pumpkin seeds

28g (1 oz) torn mozzarella cheese

Freshly ground black pepper

Method

- Preheat grill to medium

- Halve apricots & remove stones

- Put them into a bowl, add olive oil & mix well to coat

- Place apricots, cut side down, on non-stick oven pan under grill & cook until well done, approx 2 min

- Arrange rocket in a bed on a serving plate

- Sprinkle seeds over

- Scatter with mozzarella

- Sprinkle with pepper to taste

- Spread apricots round the edge & tuck into your healthy lunch

Vegetable Chilli

Ingredients

2 tbsp olive oil

½ clove garlic, crushed

½ red chilli, chopped

84g (3 oz) mushrooms, quartered

¼ tsp ground cumin

100g (3½ oz) canned chopped tomatoes

100g (3½ oz) canned kidney beans

50ml (1½ fl.oz) water

56g (2 oz) green beans, trimmed & sliced

2 tsp low-fat crème fraîche

2 wholewheat crispbreads

Method

- Heat oil in non-stick frying pan

- Add garlic & chilli & fry gently for 2 minutes

- Add mushrooms & cumin & cook for a further 3

minutes

- Pour in tomatoes, kidney beans & water

- Simmer for 10 minutes, stirring occasionally

- Mix in the green beans & cook until sauce thickens, approx 5 min

- Scoop into a serving bowl, top with crème fraîche & enjoy with the crispbreads

Poached Egg with Watercress & Tomatoes

Ingredients

1 large egg

28g (1 oz) watercress, chopped

6 cherry tomatoes, halved

1 tsp sunflower seeds

1 tsp chopped coriander

Method

- Boil a small pan of water & swirl water rapidly with a wooden spoon

- Break egg into centre of swirling water

- Cook until egg is firm, approx 2 min

- Remove egg with slotted spoon

- Place the sunflower seeds in a non-stick heated frying pan

- Cook until golden brown, keeping the pan moving to avoid burning the seeds, approx 2 min

- Mix seeds with the watercress & tomatoes & arrange on a serving plate

- Place the egg on the bed of salad & sprinkle with coriander

Spicy Balls

Ingredients

84g (3 oz) potatoes

84g (3 oz) garden peas

84g (3 oz) baby spinach

1 small green chilli

2 tsp coriander

½ tsp fresh ginger, grated

1 tbsp cornflour

2 tbsp olive oil

Salad of your choice

Method

- Peel & cut potatoes & chop spinach
- Put water on to heat & pop potatoes in when boiling
- Cook potatoes on medium heat until soft, 5 -8 min
- Meanwhile, boil another saucepan of water, add spinach & peas & cook until tender, 3-4 min

- Drain vegetables & place in a bowl

- Chop chilli & coriander finely

- Add grated ginger, chilli, coriander & cornflour to bowl

- Stir well for approx 2-3 min & mash with a fork

- Form into small, smooth balls

- Heat oil in non-stick frying pan & sauté balls, turning frequently, 3-4 min, until well cooked & lightly browned

- Transfer balls onto kitchen towel to drain

- Arrange your salad on the side of a serving plate, add the balls & enjoy while hot

Cheesy Snack

Ingredients

1 slice wholegrain bread

1 tsp crushed garlic

1 tbsp spreadable goat cheese

7g (¼ oz) spinach

1 vine tomato, sliced

¼ flesh avocado, sliced

Pinch of freshly ground pepper, to taste

Sprig of parsley

Method

- Preheat grill to medium
- Toast one side of bread
- Stir garlic into goat cheese & spread evenly over untoasted side
- Grill until just lightly browned at edges
- Transfer to serving plate

- Layer over with spinach, tomato & avocado

- Sprinkle on pepper & garnish with parsley

Tomato & Pepper Soup

Ingredients

280g (10 oz) drained roasted peppers

280g (10 oz) cherry tomatoes, halved

240ml (8 fl. oz) water

1 very low salt vegetable stock cube

1 tbsp olive oil

1 garlic clove, crushed

1 tsp paprika

Freshly ground pepper, to taste

2 tbsp ground almonds

2 basil leaves

Mixed side salad of your choice

Method

- Put all above ingredients, except side salad, into a blender
- Blend on high setting until completely smooth

- Pour into saucepan & heat, stirring frequently, until hot

- Transfer to serving bowl, pop on basil leaves & enjoy with your side salad

Potato with Cheese & Spinach Filling

Ingredients

1 large potato

100g (3½ oz) cottage cheese

Freshly ground pepper

1 tbsp olive oil

28g (1 oz) baby spinach leaves

Sprig of parsley

Method

- Pierce potato several times with a sharp knife
- Put into microwave & cook on highest setting, until soft, approx 8 min
- Scoop cheese into a bowl
- Sprinkle on pepper to taste & stir
- Heat oil in non-stick frying pan on medium heat
- Pop spinach in & cook until it begins to wilt, approx 2 min

- Add to cheese & stir

- Put potato onto serving plate & cut along length & across to open

- Top with cheese & spinach mixture

- Garnish with parsley

Easy Egg & Veg

Ingredients

2 medium potatoes, boiled

2 tbsp olive oil

2 spring onions

6 cherry tomatoes

Pinch chilli flakes

Freshly ground pepper, to taste

1 free range egg

 4 basil leaves, chopped

Method

- Slice potatoes
- Chop spring onions & basil leaves & halve tomatoes
- Heat oil in non-stick frying pan
- Sauté potatoes on medium heat on both sides until turning golden brown

- Add onions & tomatoes & fry until softened, 1-2 min

- Sprinkle with chilli flakes, season with pepper & stir

- Move veg to sides of pan leaving a space in centre for egg

- Break egg into pan & fry until cooked to your liking

- Slide contents of pan onto a plate, sprinkle with basil & serve

Pear with Cottage Cheese Snack Lunch

Ingredients

84g (3 oz) cottage cheese

2 tsp hulled pumpkin seeds (pepitas)

1 large pear

Method

- Spoon cottage cheese into a bowl & place in centre of serving plate

- Sprinkle with seeds

- Cut pear into slices & arrange around bowl

- Your snack lunch is ready!

Easy Peasy Soup

Ingredients

300ml (10 fl.oz) very low salt vegetable stock

227g (8 oz) frozen peas

Freshly ground pepper

1 tbsp natural Greek yogurt

Small sprig of mint

2 wholegrain rice cakes

Method

- Pour stock into a saucepan & bring to the boil
- Add peas, bring back to boil & simmer on low heat for 5 min, stirring occasionally
- Remove from heat & allow to cool slightly
- Season with pepper, pour into blender & whizz until smooth
- Pour into serving bowl
- Swirl in Greek yogurt
- Garnish with mint before serving with rice cakes

Spinach, Tomato, Avocado & Nut Sandwich

Ingredients

Flesh of ½ avocado

2 tsp chopped pine nuts

1 small tomato

6 baby spinach leaves

2 slices wholegrain bread

Method

- Use a fork to mash avocado in a bowl
- Add nuts & stir well
- Slice tomato & chop spinach
- Place 1 slice of bread on a plate & cover evenly with avocado mix
- Top with tomato slices
- Arrange spinach over the tomato
- Cover with the other slice of bread
- Cut in half with sharp knife & enjoy your sandwich

Quick Potassium-Rich Lunch

Ingredients

Olive oil cooking spray

1 free range egg

1 tsp water

1 tbsp chopped mushrooms

1 tbsp finely sliced baby spinach

28g (1 oz) mozzarella cheese, shredded

3 cherry tomatoes

Method

- Lightly coat microwavable bowl with oil spray
- Break egg into another bowl, add water, mushrooms & spinach & whisk thoroughly
- Pour into the oil-coated bowl
- Microwave on high setting for 20 seconds
- Stir mixture & microwave for further 30 seconds or until just set
- Sprinkle cheese on, top with tomatoes & serve

Filled Mushrooms

Ingredients

3 large mushrooms

½ tbsp chopped tomatoes

½ tbsp chopped red peppers

½ tbsp chopped olives

2 tsp finely chopped fresh parsley

¼ tsp finely chopped fresh oregano leaves

¼ tsp fresh lemon juice

½ garlic clove, crushed

Freshly ground black pepper, to taste

1 tsp olive oil

56g (2 oz) feta cheese, crumbled

3 sprigs parsley to garnish

Method

- Preheat oven to 190°C/375°F
- Lightly grease a baking tray

- Clean mushrooms with a damp piece of kitchen towel

- Remove stalks & hollow out the heads

- Put tomatoes, peppers, olives, parsley, oregano, lemon juice, garlic, pepper & oil in a bowl & stir well

- Fill mushroom heads equally & place on the baking tray

- Cook for approximately 20 minutes

- Place mushrooms on a serving plate, sprinkle each one with cheese & garnish with a sprig of parsley

Simple Savoury Sweet Salad

Ingredients

Salad:

1 large orange, segmented

112g (4 oz) strawberries, halved

56 g (2 oz) mixed salad leaves

28g (1 oz) pecan nuts, broken into pieces

Ginger & Cinnamon Dressing:

1 tbsp olive oil

1 tbsp orange juice

Tip of tsp ground ginger

Tip of tsp ground cinnamon

Freshly ground black pepper, to taste

Method

- Combine salad ingredients in a bowl
- Make the dressing, by mixing all its ingredients

together well

- Drizzle dressing over salad, toss to ensure even coating & serve

Quinoa with Vegetables

Ingredients

28g (1 oz) quinoa, uncooked

Handful broccoli florets

1 large vine tomato

Flesh of ½ avocado

Handful of kale, stripped from stems

Handful of baby spinach

¼ chilli

¼ lemon

1 tsp olive oil

Freshly ground black pepper

Method

- Rinse quinoa & cook according to instructions on packet

- While it's cooking, steam broccoli until tender but crunchy, approx 4 – 5 min & drain

- Cut tomato into quarters

- Cut avocado flesh into cubes

- Slice kale, spinach & chilli finely

- Put cooked quinoa into a large bowl

- Add all the vegetables

- Squeeze lemon over

- Drizzle with oil & season with pepper

- Toss thoroughly & serve with a satisfied smile

Spicy Tomato & Aubergine

Ingredients

1 small onion

4 tbsp olive oil

1 chilli, chopped finely

200g (7 oz) can chopped tomatoes

1 aubergine

2 tsp chopped basil leaves

Pinch of freshly ground pepper

Wholemeal roll

Method

- Cut onion & aubergine into slices & chop chilli finely

- Heat 2 tbsp of the oil in a non-stick pan

- Cook onion slices until softened on medium heat

- Add chilli & cook until just tender

- Tip in tomatoes with juice, bring to boiling point then turn heat to low & simmer for 10 min

- Whilst mixture is simmering, heat rest of oil in another non-stick pan

- Add aubergine & cook over gentle heat until golden brown

- Turn slices over & continue cooking as above until slices are cooked & tender

- Slide them onto a warm plate

- Add basil to tomato & onion mixture

- Spoon mixture over aubergine slices & enjoy with the tasty wholemeal roll

Beetroot Hummus with Veggie Sticks

Ingredients

1 tsp olive oil

½ small clove of garlic, crushed

28g (1 oz) cooked beetroot, chopped

42g (1½ oz) canned chickpeas, rinsed & drained

¼ tsp ground coriander

¼ tsp ground cumin

Freshly ground black pepper

2 tsp lemon juice, freshly squeezed

½ small pepper, sliced into sticks

1 small carrot, peeled & sliced into sticks

¼ cucumber, peeled & cut into sticks

1 stem of celery, cut into sticks

Method

- Put oil, garlic, beetroot, chickpeas, coriander, cumin, ground pepper & lemon juice into a food processor, & blend until you get a smooth hummus consistency

- Scoop beetroot hummus into a bowl, place in centre of a serving plate & surround with veggie sticks

- Dip to your heart's content!

Simple Mozzarella Salad

Ingredients

84g (3 oz) rocket

1 large vine tomato

Flesh of ½ avocado

3 slices Mozzarella cheese

6 basil leaves

Dressing:

2 tsp balsamic vinegar

1 tbsp olive oil

½ tsp pure runny honey

Freshly ground black pepper

Method

- Place rocket in a medium-sized serving bowl
- Slice tomato & avocado & add to bowl
- Top with Mozzarella

- Tear basil leaves & scatter over

- Mix vinegar, oil, honey & pepper thoroughly in a small bowl to make dressing

- Pour over salad & toss well to coat

Figs, Cottage Cheese & Walnuts

Ingredients

2 figs

84g (3oz) cottage cheese

28g (1 oz) walnuts

Method

- Chop figs
- Break walnuts into pieces
- Scoop cottage cheese into serving bowl
- Stir figs into cottage cheese
- Sprinkle walnuts over & relish each mouthful

Dinners

Warming Lentils & Vegetables

Ingredients

2 tbsp olive oil

70g (2½ oz) onion

42g (1½ oz) carrot

42g (1½ oz) celery

60ml (2 fl.oz) water

200g (7 oz) canned chopped tomatoes

200g (7 oz) canned lentils, rinsed & drained

6g (¼ oz) fresh parsley, chopped

Freshly ground pepper

Method

- Chop onion, carrot & celery

- Heat oil in a non-stick frying pan

- Fry onion, carrot & celery for approx 4 min, until veg is soft

- Add water, tomatoes with juice, lentils, parsley & pepper & slowly bring to the boil over medium heat

- Lower heat, cover & simmer for 10 min, or until most of the liquid is absorbed, stirring occasionally, then serve

Chilli Non Carne

Ingredients

70g (2½ oz) brown rice

1 tbsp olive oil

1 clove garlic

½ small onion

56g (2 oz) meat-free mince

1 tsp chilli powder

240ml (8 fl.oz) water

3 tbsp canned chopped tomato with juice

2 tsp pure tomato purée

Pinch of freshly ground black pepper

1 very low salt vegetable stock cube

½ small can kidney beans

42g (1½ oz) frozen garden peas

Method

- Put rice on to cook according to instructions on

packet

- While rice is cooking, chop garlic finely & slice onion thinly

- Heat oil in a non-stick frying pan

- When oil is hot, fry garlic & onion on medium to high heat for approx 3 min until tender

- Add mince & chilli powder & stir-fry for 1-2 min

- Add water, tomatoes, tomato purée & pepper

- Crush stock cube, add & stir thoroughly until mixture reaches boiling point

- Simmer for 20 min, stirring frequently

- Add kidney beans, cover & simmer for a further 5 min

- Put peas into a small microwavable bowl with 1 tbsp water & cook in microwave for approx 2 min until piping hot

- Drain rice & transfer to serving plate

- Spoon chilli mixture onto bed of rice

- Drain peas & sprinkle over

- Serve & enjoy!

Roasted Squash Risotto

Ingredients

1 small onion

250g (9 oz) butternut squash

3 tbsp olive oil

¾ tsp dried red chilli flakes

Freshly ground black pepper, to taste

75g (2½ oz) risotto rice

60ml (2 fl.oz) dry white wine

420ml (14 fl.oz) very low salt vegetable stock

28g (1 oz) grated vegetarian parmesan-style cheese

14g (½ oz) pumpkin seeds

1 tbsp crème fraîche

Method

- Preheat oven to 230°C/450°F
- Peel, de-seed & dice squash

- Chop onion finely

- Put squash into a bowl, add 1 tbsp oil & ¼ tsp chilli flakes

- Season with pepper & mix thoroughly to coat squash

- Transfer to a small, foil-lined roasting tin & roast for approx 20 min until golden, turning occasionally

- Meanwhile, heat 1 tbsp oil in frying pan, add onion & saute for 1 min

- Add rice & stir continuously for 2 min over gentle heat

- Stir in the wine & simmer until almost absorbed

- Add stock gradually, pouring in a little more each time it gets absorbed, stirring continuously until rice is cooked & tender

- Remove from heat, add squash & cheese & mix well

- Heat 1 tbsp oil in frying pan, add rest of chilli flakes & pumpkin seeds & toast for 1-2 min

- Spoon rice & squash mix onto plate & sprinkle with flakes & seeds

- Top with crème fraîche to serve

Mixed Veg Casserole

Ingredients

2 tbsp olive oil

1 small onion

56g (2 oz) swede

56g (2 oz) parsnip

100g (3½ oz) sweet potato, peeled

1 small stick celery

1 medium carrot

56g (2 oz) sliced mushrooms

6 small cauliflower florets

180ml (6 fl.oz) very low salt vegetable stock

1 tbsp pure tomato purée

1 tsp mixed herbs

1 bay leaf

1 slice wholemeal crusty bread

Method

- Preheat oven to 180°C/350°F

- Heat oil in frying pan & sauté onion until it begins to turn golden brown

- Transfer to casserole dish

- Peel & chop swede, parsnip, potato, celery & carrot & add to casserole

- Add mushrooms & cauliflower

- Stir tomato purée into the boiling stock until dissolved then pour onto vegetables

- Pop in the bay leaf & stir in the herbs

- Cover & cook for approx 1 hour until potato is tender

- Serve with a slice of wholemeal crusty bread

Lentil & Vegetable Couscous

Ingredients

75g (2½ oz) couscous

120ml (4 fl.oz) boiling water

2 tbsp olive oil

125g (4½ oz) frozen grilled vegetable mix

200g (7 oz) canned lentils, rinsed & drained

Freshly ground black pepper

6g (¼ oz) chopped parsley

Method

- Put couscous into a bowl, pour boiling water onto it & cover with clingfilm

- After 5 min, or water is absorbed, fluff with fork

- Heat oil in non-stick frying pan & fry veg for approx 3 min, until softened

- Stir in lentils & cook for 2 min

- Stir in couscous & season with pepper

- Transfer to a serving bowl & sprinkle parsley over to garnish

Mixed Bean Salad

Ingredients

400g (14 oz) can of mixed beans

1 large trimmed spring onion

2 large tomatoes

¼ cucumber

2 tbsp chopped parsley

1 tsp olive oil

Freshly ground black pepper, to taste

1 tsp lemon juice

1 tsp toasted sesame seeds

1 slice crusty wholegrain bread

Method

- Drain & rinse beans & put into a medium-sized serving bowl

- Chop spring onion, tomatoes & cucumber into small chunks

- Add to beans, together with parsley, oil, pepper & lemon juice

- Stir well to combine

- Sprinkle evenly with sesame seeds & enjoy with crusty bread

Spicy Pasta Spirals with Courgette

Ingredients

100g (3½ oz) pasta spirals

1 large courgette

1 tsp olive oil

¼ fresh red chilli, de-seeded

Zest of ½ lemon

1 tsp lemon juice

1 tbsp freshly chopped basil

Freshly ground black pepper

Sprig of parsley

Method

- Cook pasta spirals according to instructions on packet

- Grate courgette

- When pasta is cooked, drain & put back into saucepan

- Add courgette & remaining ingredients

- Warm mixture thoroughly on low heat, stirring continuously

- Transfer to warmed serving bowl

- Garnish with parsley

- Eat before it cools down

Nutty Spicy Baked Sweet Potato

Ingredients

1 large sweet potato

56g (2 oz) unsalted cashew nuts

3¼ tsp olive oil

1 tsp lemon juice

Freshly ground black pepper

56g (2 oz) sweet corn, canned or frozen

112g (4 oz) canned black beans, drained

¼ tsp paprika

¼ tsp cumin

¼ tsp chilli powder

28g (1 oz) baby spinach, chopped

1 tbsp chopped coriander

Juice of ½ lime

2 small sprigs parsley

Method

- Preheat oven to 200°C/400°F

- Bake potato for approx 1 hour, until soft when pierced

- Put nuts, ¼ tsp oil, lemon juice & pepper into a food processor & whizz until nuts are crumbled

- Heat rest of oil in a large frying pan

- Add corn & cook gently for 1 min until just brown

- Add beans & spices & cook, whilst stirring, for 3 min

- Stir in spinach & coriander & cook until they wilt

- Halve potato & top each half with corn & beans

- Top each one with nut mixture, squeeze lime juice over, garnish with parsley & tuck in!

Dressed Lentils with Cherries & Rocket

Ingredients

225g (8 oz) cooked green lentils, rinsed & drained

170g (6 oz) cherries

Generous handful of rocket

For vinaigrette:

1 tbsp lemon juice

½ tsp Dijon mustard

3 tbsp olive oil

1 tsp honey

1 small garlic clove, crushed

Freshly ground black pepper

Method

- Put all ingredients for vinaigrette into a sealed container & shake vigorously
- Put lentils into a serving bowl

- Quarter cherries (stones removed)

- Add cherries & rocket to lentils

- Drizzle on vinaigrette, to taste, & mix well before serving

Pasta with Courgette, Onion & Pepper

Ingredients

100g (3½ oz) pasta shapes

1 courgette

1 red onion

1 yellow pepper

1 tbsp olive oil

Freshly ground black pepper

1 tsp freshly chopped parsley

Method

- Preheat oven to 200°C/400°F

- Peel & cut courgette & onion into chunks

- De-seed pepper & cut into chunks

- Put all veg into a foil-lined roasting tin, coat thoroughly with oil & season with pepper

- Roast for approx 30 min, until tender, turning occasionally

- Meanwhile, cook pasta according to instructions on packet

- Once cooked, rinse pasta with boiling water, drain, return to pan & cover

- Add veg to pasta & mix well

- Scoop into serving bowl & sprinkle with parsley to serve

Baked Potato with Broccoli, Cheese & Salad

Ingredients

1 medium sweet potato

4 florets broccoli

56g (2 oz) low fat cheddar cheese, grated

Chopped chives to taste

Salad of your choice

Method

- Preheat oven to 350°C/180°F

- Pierce potato several times with a sharp knife

- Put into microwave & cook on highest setting, until soft, approx 8 min

- Meanwhile, prepare your salad

- Halve potato lengthwise & top each half with broccoli

- Sprinkle with cheese & place in oven on foil-lined baking tray

- Bake for approx 10 min until cheese is melted & golden brown

- Sprinkle with chives & serve with salad

Tomatoes, Beans & Cauliflower

Ingredients

56g (2 oz) green beans

½ cauliflower

1 small onion

2 tomatoes

1 tbsp oil

1 tsp cumin seeds

100g (3½ oz) canned butter beans, drained

30ml (1 fl.oz) water

10g ($^1/_3$ oz) coriander, chopped

Method

- Trim beans & slice in half lengthways

- Break cauliflower into florets

- Slice onion & dice tomatoes

- Put cauliflower into a saucepan of boiling water & cook for 3 min

- Add green beans & cook for 2 more min, then drain

- Meanwhile heat the oil in non-stick frying pan

- Put onion & cumin seeds into hot oil & fry gently for approx 2 min, until soft

- Stir in tomatoes, butter beans & water & continue cooking for 2 min until well heated through

- Put green beans & cauliflower into a serving bowl

- Add tomatoes, butter bean mixture & coriander

- Stir well & it's ready!

Oriental Tofu Curry

Ingredients

84g (3 oz) extra firm tofu, drained & pressed

2 tbsp olive oil

1 onion

56g (2 oz) baby spinach leaves

¼ cucumber

5 tsp green curry paste

1 garlic clove, minced

¼ tsp cumin

170g (6 oz) cauliflower florets

240ml (8 fl.oz) light coconut milk

28g (1 oz) chopped mint

¼ lime

Green salad

Method

- Chop onion & spinach & slice cucumber

- Cut tofu into cubes

- Heat oil in lidded non-stick frying pan & fry tofu gently until golden brown, approx 4 min

- Remove from pan & pat dry on paper towel

- Fry onion for approx 3 min, until soft

- Add curry paste, garlic & cumin & cook for 1 min, stirring continuously

- Add cauliflower, stir in coconut milk & bring to boil

- Cover & simmer for 10 min

- Add spinach, stir & cook for 2 min

- Add tofu cubes & mint & stir well

- Scoop into a serving bowl, leaving space to put cucumber alongside

- Squeeze lime over cucumber & serve with a green salad

Quinoa with Vegetables & Nuts

Ingredients

28g (1 oz) quinoa

4 broccoli florets

Small handful baby spinach leaves

¼ red pepper

½ avocado

3 cherry tomatoes

Juice of ¼ lemon

1 tsp olive oil

Freshly ground black pepper

1 tsp chopped mixed nuts

Method

- Rinse quinoa thoroughly
- Tip quinoa into a saucepan & add double its volume of water
- Bring to boil over medium heat

- Simmer for approx 10 - 15 min until tender & water is absorbed

- While quinoa is cooking, steam broccoli for approx 5 min until heated through but crunchy

- Thinly slice spinach, pepper, avocado & halve tomatoes

- Put cooked quinoa into a bowl & add vegetables

- Sprinkle with lemon juice, olive oil, pepper & nuts

- Enjoy your meal!

Stuffed Peppers

Ingredients

2 large peppers, 1 red, 1 yellow

84g (3 oz) quinoa

6 cherry tomatoes

1 clove garlic, minced

140g (5 oz) canned chickpeas, drained

2 tbsp pine nuts

1 tbsp sliced black olives

1 tsp red wine vinegar

1 tsp dried oregano

1 tbsp freshly chopped parsley

Method

- Preheat oven to 150°C /300°F

- Rinse quinoa & cook according to instructions on packet

- Cut peppers into halves, remove stems & seeds

- Place peppers on foil-lined baking tray

- Cut tomatoes into quarters & put into a bowl

- Add cooked quinoa, garlic, chickpeas, pine nuts, olives, vinegar & oregano & mix until thoroughly combined

- Scoop mixture into pepper halves

- Bake in oven for approx 20 min, until peppers are cooked but still firm

- Transfer peppers to a serving plate, sprinkle with parsley & serve

Spicy Peas & Mushrooms with Naan Bread

Ingredients

1 small onion

140g (5 oz) button mushrooms

2 tbsp olive oil

84g (3 oz) frozen peas

100ml (3½ fl.oz) masala sauce

¼ tsp chilli powder

¼ tsp ground cumin

¼ tsp turmeric

¼ tsp garam masala

¼ tsp fenugreek powder

1 tsp freshly chopped coriander

1 naan bread

Method

- Chop onion & slice mushrooms.

- Heat oil in a wok.

- Add onion & mushrooms & cook, whilst stirring, for 4 minutes

- Add peas & cook for a further 2 min

- Stir in the masala sauce until simmering

- Mix in chilli, cumin & turmeric

- Simmer for 10 min, stirring occasionally, adding a small amount of water, as necessary, to avoid mixture becoming too thick

- Add garam masala & fenugreek powder, stir well & simmer for 5 min

- Cover naan bread with moist kitchen towel & heat in microwave for approx 20 seconds

- Scoop mixture onto a serving plate, garnish with coriander & eat with naan bread

Pasta with Goat Cheese, Asparagus & Tomato

Ingredients

75g (2½ oz) wholewheat pasta spirals

56g (2 oz) chopped asparagus

2 tsp water

56g (2 oz) cherry tomatoes, halved

1 small clove garlic, minced

28g (1 oz) chopped fresh basil

 Freshly ground black pepper to taste

28g (1 oz) goat cheese

Method

- Cook pasta spirals according to directions on packet

- While pasta is cooking, put asparagus & water into microwavable bowl

- Microwave on high setting for approx 3 min, until asparagus is tender

- Drain pasta & transfer to serving bowl

- Add tomatoes, basil, garlic, pepper, asparagus & goat cheese

- Toss to mix & serve

Quorn Vegetable Stew

Ingredients

Olive oil cooking spray

84g (3 oz) Quorn pieces

1 small onion

1 small green pepper

½ clove garlic

½ tsp paprika

200g (7 oz) can of chopped tomatoes

½ tsp dried oregano

½ tsp pure tomato purée

60ml (2 fl.oz) red wine

Pinch of stevia

Freshly ground black pepper

1 medium potato

Method

- Slice onion, pepper & garlic thinly

- Peel & chop potato, put in saucepan of cold water & cook, then drain & cover

- Coat lidded frying pan with olive oil & heat

- Fry onion until soft

- Add Quorn & sliced pepper.

- Cook for 5 min, stirring continuously, until pepper softens

- Stir in garlic & paprika

- Stir in tomatoes with juice

- Add oregano, purée, wine, stevia & ground pepper & stir well

- Bring to boil, then lower heat, cover & simmer for 15 minutes, stirring occasionally.

- Once liquid begins to thicken, stir in drained potato & cook for a further 4 min

- Transfer to serving plate

- Enjoy!

Onion, Spinach, Black Bean & Pumpkin Curry

Ingredients

1 small onion thinly sliced

200g (7 oz) peeled pumpkin

1 tbsp olive oil

1 small garlic clove, crushed

½ tsp ground cumin

½ tsp ground coriander

½ tsp curry powder

Small pinch of chilli powder

2 tsp pure tomato purée

210ml (7 fl.oz) boiling water

200g (7 oz) canned black beans, drained & rinsed

100g (3 ½ oz) spinach

1 naan bread

Method

- Preheat oven to 190°C /375°F

- Slice onion & cut peeled pumpkin into chunks

- Heat oil in non-stick frying pan then fry onion until just golden

- Stir in garlic & all spices & cook for 1 more min

- Add pumpkin, boiling water & tomato purée & bring to the boil, stirring continuously

- Lower heat cover & simmer for 15 min, stirring frequently

- Add beans & cook for 5 min, stirring often

- Pour a kettle of boiling water over spinach until it wilts & drain well, pressing with spoon to remove as much water as possible

- Chop spinach & stir it into the curry, mixing well to combine

- Spoon curry onto a serving plate & enjoy with warmed naan bread

Baked Potato with Lentils & Kale

Ingredients

1 large baking potato

56g (2 oz) dried lentils

180ml (6 fl.oz) water

1 tbsp olive oil

2 large kale leaves

1 garlic clove, minced

Freshly ground black pepper

1 tsp natural fat free yogurt

1 tbsp chopped parsley

Method

- Preheat oven to 200°C/400°F
- Wash & pierce potato several times
- Bake potato for approx 1 hour, until soft inside
- Meanwhile, put lentils & water in a saucepan & heat until boiling

- Turn heat to low, cover & simmer for approx 15 min, stirring occasionally, until lentils have absorbed the water

- Remove stems & slice kale into strips

- Heat oil in a non-stick frying pan on medium heat

- Add kale & garlic & cook for approx 2 min, whilst stirring, until kale wilts

- Stir in lentils & turn off heat

- Slice potato lengthwise to form an open pocket

- Scoop lentil & kale mix into pocket & top with yogurt

- Sprinkle with pepper to taste & garnish with parsley before serving

Veggie Biryani

Ingredients

3 tbsp rice

2 tbsp olive oil

112g (4 oz) onion

1 small carrot

4 cardamom pods

½ tsp cumin seeds

¼ tsp cinnamon

84g (3 oz) frozen peas

1 tbsp lemon juice

120 ml water

1 clove garlic

1 tsp freshly grated ginger

1 tsp pure tomato purée

½ tsp paprika

¼ tsp turmeric

1 tbsp chopped tomatoes

100ml (3½ fl.oz) water

4 large mushrooms

Method

- Chop onion & garlic finely
- Chop carrot lengthwise into thin strips
- De-seed cardamom pods
- Chop mushrooms
- Thoroughly rinse rice & drain
- Pre-heat oven to 170°C/325°F
- Heat oil in a non-stick, lidded frying pan & fry onion for approx 3 min until tender
- Stir in cardamom & cumin seeds
- Add cinnamon & stir again
- Simmer for 6 min, stirring occasionally
- Stir in the rice, peas, lemon juice & water & heat to boiling point
- Cover with lid & simmer for 5 min.
- Stir rice & continue to cook, covered, for 3 min

- Transfer rice mixture to an oven-proof dish & cook in oven for 15 min

- Meanwhile, heat oil in a wok & fry the onion with the carrot for approx 3 min until softened, stirring continuously

- Add garlic, ginger & tomato purée & continue cooking for a further min, whilst stirring

- Stir in paprika & turmeric

- Add chopped tomatoes & 100ml water.

- Simmer for 5 min, stirring frequently

- Add mushrooms & continue simmering & stirring for 5 min, adding a small amount of water if sauce starts to dry out too much

- Remove rice from oven, spoon it into the sauce, stir & heat through

- Scoop mixture onto serving plate & savour the flavours

Quorn Cottage Pie

Ingredients

2 tbsp olive oil

70g (2½ oz) carrot

56g (2 oz) celery

125g (4½ oz) onion

2 medium potatoes, quartered

56g (2 oz) Quorn mince

1 tsp plain flour

210 ml (7 fl.oz) boiling water

1 very low salt vegetable stock cube

1 tsp chopped parsley

2 tsp pure tomato purée

½ tsp mixed herbs

Freshly ground black pepper

1 tsp mustard powder

84g (3 oz) frozen garden peas

Method

- Preheat oven to 200°C/400°F

- Finely chop carrot, celery & onion

- Grease an ovenproof dish.

- Put potatoes on to boil

- Heat oil in non-stick frying pan

- Add carrot, celery & onion & cook until onion is soft.

- Add mince & cook for 2 min

- Stir flour into mince & vegetables.

- Add water & stir in crumbled stock cube

- Stir in the parsley & tomato purée.

- Season with black pepper & mixed herbs

- Simmer for 15 min

- When potatoes have cooked, mash them with a little olive oil spread & low fat milk & season to taste.

- When mince & vegetables are cooked, mix in mustard powder.

- Spoon mince mixture into oven dish

- Cover evenly with mashed potato

- Bake in the oven for 20 min

- Put peas in microwavable bowl with 1 tbsp water, cover & microwave for 2 min

- Drain & spoon peas onto side of a serving plate

- Add cottage pie

- Bon appetit!

Tempting Tofu

Ingredients

140g (5 oz) firm tofu

112g (4 oz) onion, diced

¼ tsp garlic powder

112g (4 oz) grated carrot

1 small red pepper

1 small courgette

Olive oil cooking spray

Freshly ground black pepper

½ tsp cumin

¼ tsp turmeric

¼ tsp smoked paprika

¼ tsp curry power

Large handful of spinach

1 tsp sesame seeds

1 tsp chopped coriander

Method

- Drain, rinse, press, dry & crumble tofu

- Dice onion, peel & grate carrot

- De-seed & dice pepper

- Peel & dice courgette

- Coat a lidded non-stick frying pan well with oil & heat on medium temperature

- When hot, add onion & garlic powder & cook for 2 - 3 min, until onion is soft

- Stir tofu into onion

- Cook for a further 3 - 5 min until just brown, stirring occasionally

- Stir in grated carrot, red pepper & courgette & season with black pepper.

- Sauté for 4 min, stirring frequently

- Mix in the spices & cook for approx 3 min, until veg is tender

- Add spinach & cook for 1 min then turn heat to low, cover pan & cook for approx 2 min, until spinach wilts

- Transfer to a serving plate

- Sprinkle with sesame seeds, scatter coriander over & your meal is ready to enjoy

Courgetti with Tomatoes & Perfect Pesto

Ingredients

8 baby plum tomatoes

1 tbsp balsamic vinegar

1 small garlic clove, crushed

Freshly ground black pepper

2 tbsp olive oil

280g (10 oz) courgetti

2 tbsp homemade vegetarian pesto (see below)

1 tbsp toasted pine nuts

Sprig of parsley

Home-made salt-free pesto:

42g (1½ oz) pine nuts

3 tbsp olive oil

1 clove garlic

40g (1½ oz) basil leaves

Juice of ¼ lemon

Pinch of freshly ground black pepper

Method

To make pesto:

- Put nuts, oil & garlic into a blender & blend for a few secs to break up nuts & garlic

- Add basil, lemon juice & pepper & blend until you get a smooth, thick paste

- If desired, add a little more lemon juice & pepper

Courgetti & Tomatoes:

- Cut 4 of the tomatoes into halves

- Put 1 tsp olive oil, the vinegar, garlic & pepper into a bowl, season with pepper & mix well

- Add all tomatoes & toss to coat thoroughly

- Heat 1 tbsp oil in non-stick frying pan

- Put tomatoes into hot oil & cook for approx 5 min, stirring frequently, until whole tomatoes begin to burst

- Put courgetti into a sieve, pour a kettle of boiling water over & drain thoroughly

- Put into a serving bowl, add pesto & toss well

- Stir in tomatoes

- Heat in microwave for about 1 minute until well heated through

- Stir well

- Sprinkle with pine nuts & garnish with parsley

Speedy Spinach All'Italiana

Ingredients

56g (2 oz) dry spaghetti

10g ($^1/_3$ oz) spinach leaves

1 large garlic clove

2 tbsp fresh parsley, finely chopped

2 tbsp olive oil

Small pinch of red pepper flakes

Method

- Cook spaghetti according to instructions on packet
- While it's cooking, slice garlic thinly & chop spinach
- Heat oil in a non-stick frying pan on medium heat
- Add garlic & red pepper flakes & sauté for approx 2 min
- Drain spaghetti & mix into garlic & flakes
- Stir in spinach & parsley & cook for a further 2 min
- Serve immediately

Index of Recipes

Breakfasts

Lunches

Dinners

Printed in Great Britain
by Amazon

16024572R00088